Wee WICKEDS Coloring Book

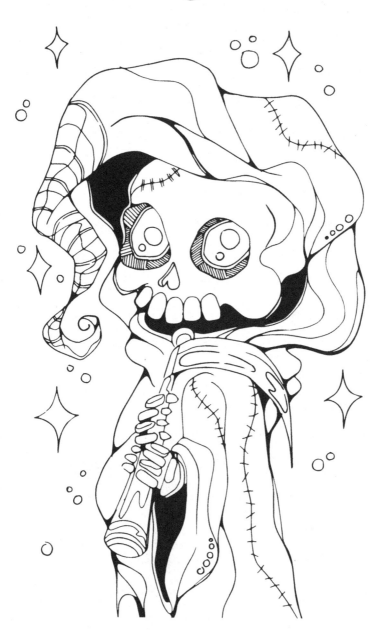

illustrated by Karla Magaña

Copyright © 2018 Karla Magaña

All rights reserved. No part of this publication may be reproduced, distributed, or transmitted in any form or by any means, including photocopying, recording, or other electronic or mechanical methods without the prior written permission of the creator, except for purposes of review and other non-commercial uses permitted by copyright law. DON'T BE A JERK!

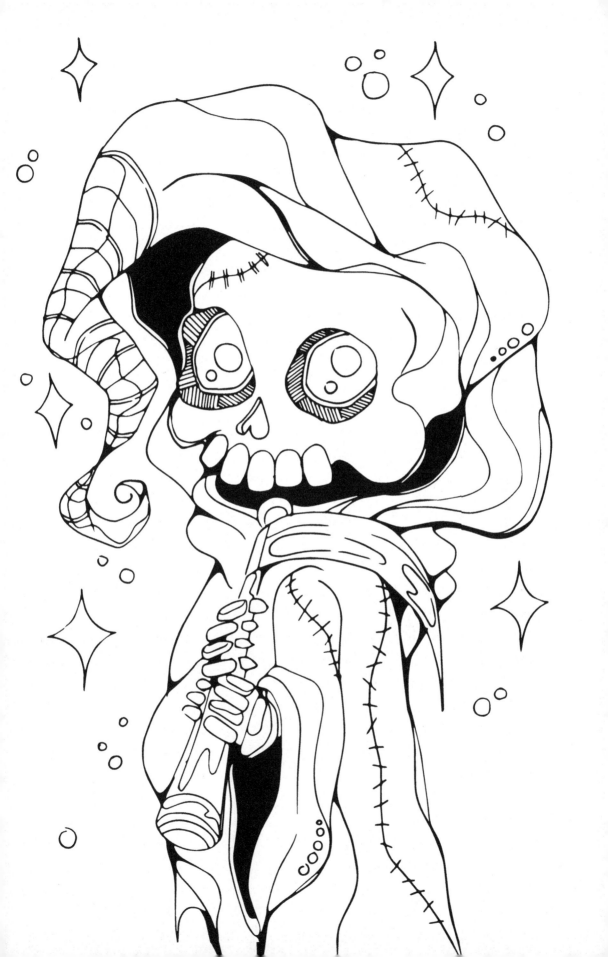

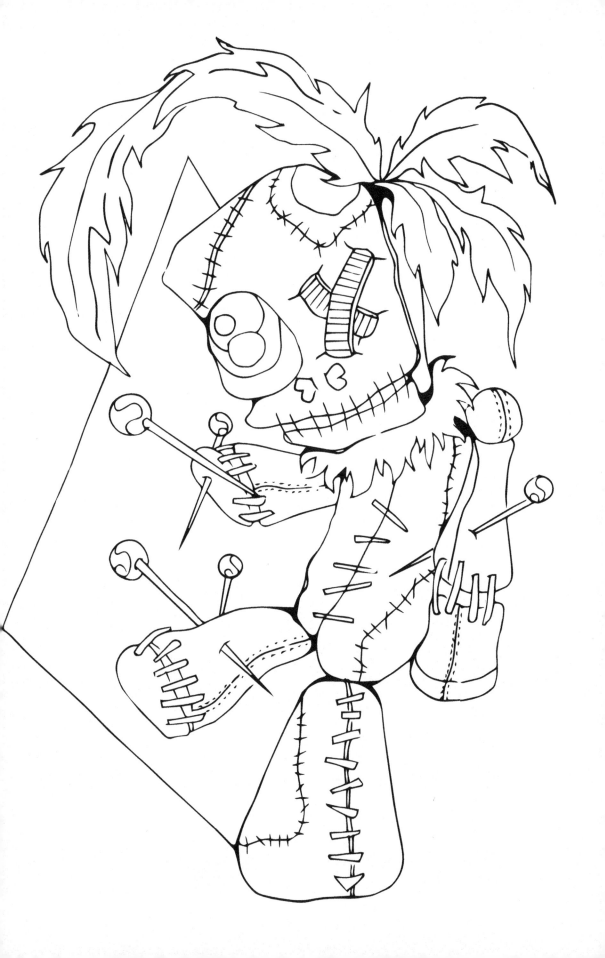

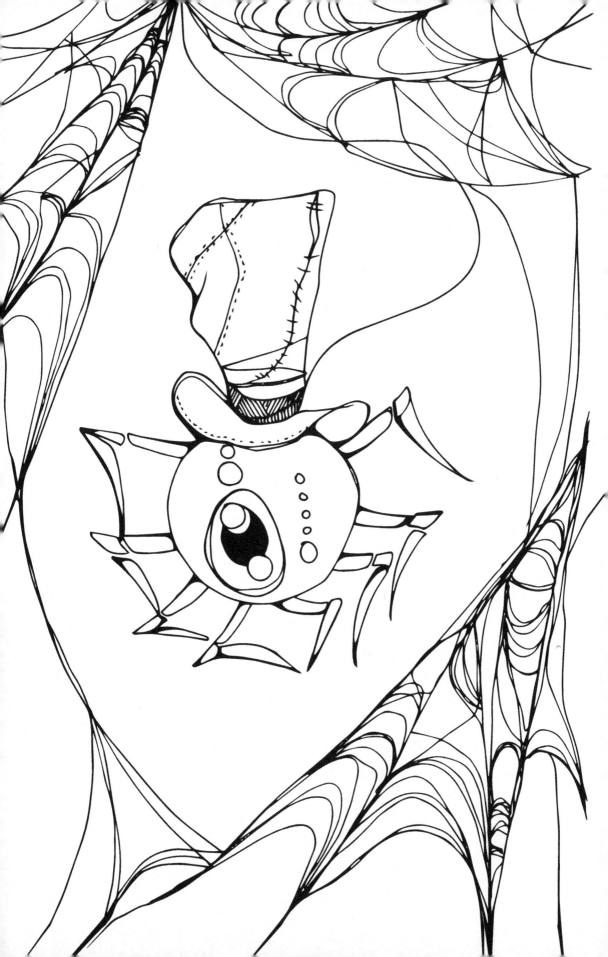

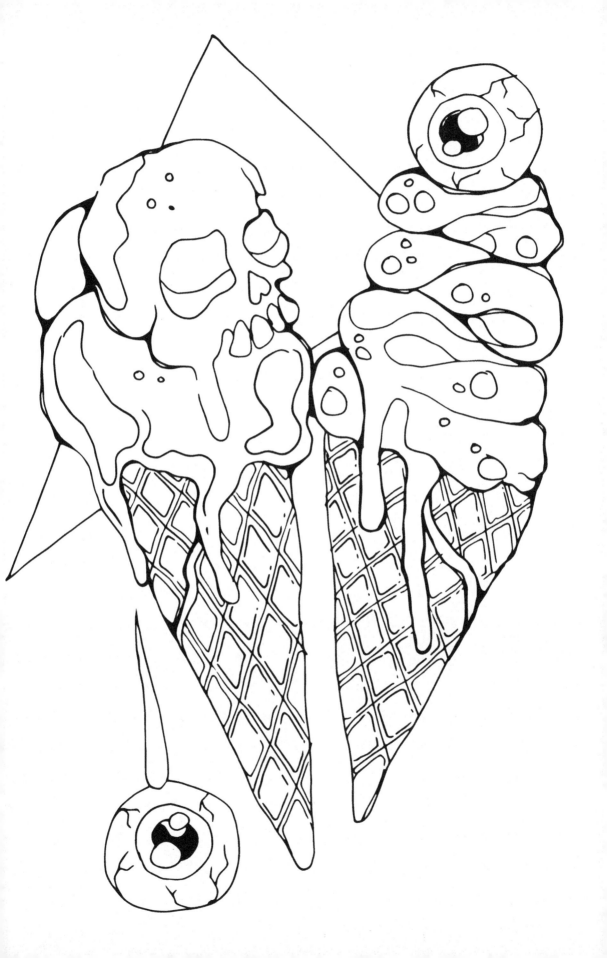

Test your supplies here ...

... and here

JOIN ME ONLINE

FACEBOOK | artistkarlamagana
INSTAGRAM | karla_magana

#WeeWickedsColoringBook
-and/or-
#Karlaween

to share your pages!

ALSO AVAILABLE

KARLAMAGANA.COM

Made in the USA
Columbia, SC
23 December 2024